The Railways of Camden

by K A Scholey

Edited by F Peter Woodford

Designed by Ivor Kamlish

© Camden History Society 2002
ISBN 0 904491 53 6

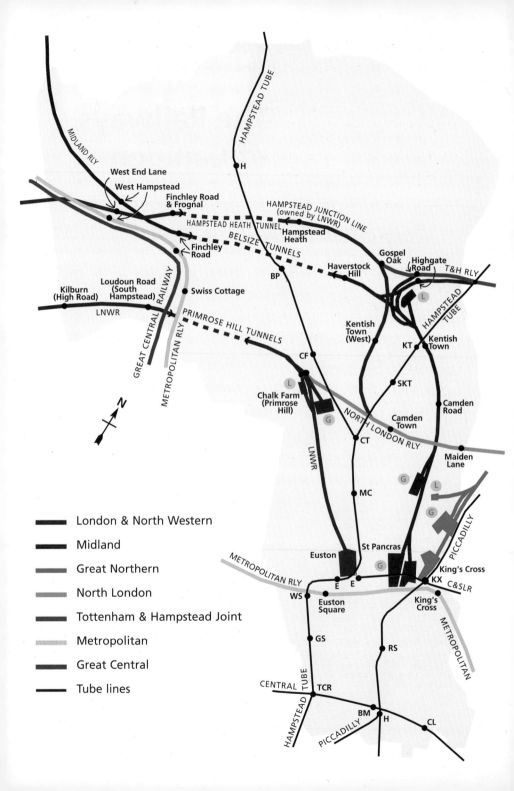

Ownership of railway lines in 1914
(present Borough of Camden represented by the grey background)

Coloured lines show the main railway companies or lines operating in 1914. Letters in circles denote G = goods depot or yard, L = locomotive depot. Names of stations on these railways are inscribed in full. The West Hampstead and Swiss Cottage stations on the 'Met.' Railway were later transferred to the Jubilee (Tube) Line (1979).

Black lines denote Underground lines, with stations abbreviated thus:

from north to south within the Borough on the present Northern Line:

H = Hampstead
BP = Belsize Park   KT = Kentish Town
CF = Chalk Farm   (SKT = South Kentish Town, defunct)

CT = Camden Town

MC = Mornington Crescent
E = Euston   E = Euston (City & S London Railway)
WS = Warren Street   KX = King's Cross
GS = Goodge Street
TCR = Tottenham Court Road

from north to south on the Piccadilly Line:

KX = King's Cross
RS = Russell Square
H = Holborn

from west to east on the Central Line
(then known as the Central London Railway):

TCR = Tottenham Court Road
(BM = British Museum, closed)
H = Holborn
CL = Chancery Lane

Illustrations

Contents

1 Introduction

From a railway historian's point of view the London Borough of Camden has a greater range of significant features than almost any other area of London. The area contains three important railway termini, sections of four main lines, parts of two vital cross-city goods and passenger links, numerous underground lines, three huge goods depots and a similar number of engine sheds.

This Occasional Paper provides chronological and technical information about railways in the area and attempts to explain their geographical configuration. The emphasis is on physical features, especially stations, rather than on services or rolling stock.

A few short notes about general railway history might be a useful starting-point. Britain's railways had their origins as commercial ventures.

By the time of WW I there were over a hundred private railway companies. These were referred to by shortened versions of their full title (for example, the London & North Western became the "North Western") or by their initials (e.g. LNWR). In 1923 the companies were reorganised by the government into four large groups of railways, which remained private concerns. These were the Great Western (GWR), Southern (SR), London, Midland & Scottish (LMS) and London & North Eastern (LNER) Railways. In 1948 the almost bankrupt railway companies were brought into State ownership. *British Railways*, as the nationalised network was termed, lasted until privatisation in the mid-1990s.

In Camden the following companies are important (see also diagram on p 2):

name	initials	terminus	After 1923
Great Central Railway	GCR	Marylebone	LNER
Great Eastern Railway*	GER	Liverpool Street	LNER
Great Northern Railway	GNR	King's Cross	LNER
London & North Western Railway	LNWR	Euston	LMS
Midland Railway	MR	St Pancras	LMS
North London Railway	NLR	Broad Street	(to LNWR 1922)

* Entered Camden only as joint owner (with Midland) of Tottenham & Hampstead Joint Railway.

2 The main-line termini

The outstanding feature of the three termini in Camden is their proximity. King's Cross and St Pancras are virtually next-door neighbours [1], while Euston is just 5 minutes' walk away down Euston Road. One reason for this is that the three owning companies were in competition, particularly over the route to Scotland. As every Business Studies graduate knows, proximity is a key element of competition – if you set up a greengrocer's shop you should position it near other greengrocers to take away their trade. It may well be asked why the railway companies did not agree to share one large 'Union Station', in the American fashion. This arrangement had been tried by the Midland, who ran trains into Euston between 1846 and 1857 and into King's Cross between 1857 and 1868. In both cases bickering and growth of traffic undermined the deal – the management of each railway company wanted an independent terminus to cash in on the certainty of passenger receipts to and from the capital without the financial and operational complexities of arrangements with another company.

The main reason for the Euston Road line-up, however, is economic and has to do with the type of land and its ownership. At the start of the railway age the area north of the Euston Road was almost entirely free

1   Aerial view of King's Cross (above) and St Pancras stations, c.1926

of buildings, and most existing buildings were of poor quality. The low value of this land made it easy for the London & Birmingham

Railway to purchase it for railway use. The Great Northern came in at King's Cross more than a decade later but the same conditions applied, and the area was already established as a railway area, unsuitable for better-quality developments. Land prices remained lower than in the rest of London, which enabled the Midland Railway to buy land sufficient not only for its passenger terminus but for a large goods depot too. There were few ground landlords; this favoured purchase by the railway companies, avoiding legal complications and saving time. The story of how the Midland could buy the Agar estate for very little, demolish Agar Town, displacing its total population, and be lauded for it in the public press has been told by Steven Denford in Camden History Society's *Occasional Paper No.1* (1995).

Political factors in this process in the early Victorian era were relatively unimportant. It is true that Euston Road (the New Road) was set as the boundary of railway development by the government in 1846, but a move southward over Bloomsbury (the Bedford Estate) and the area east of Bloomsbury (smaller estates owned by several influential bodies such as the Skinners and the Foundling Hospital) would in any case have been hugely costly. During the 1860s the government did authorise an underground line down Tottenham Court Road to link Charing Cross with Euston, but this was abandoned in the financial crisis of 1866. And the poorest folk who occupied the slums and near slums north of Euston Road (including Agar Town) had no political voice, since at this time they had no vote.

What of 20th-century developments? Although the competitive companies had found it difficult to share facilities, the earlier conditions did not apply after 1923 – and particularly after 1948. Why did not the 'Grouped' companies or the nationalised network combine the stations (for example, concentrating on Euston or King's Cross the traffic into St Pancras)? First, neither the Grouped companies nor British Railways possessed the dynamic leadership needed for such radical change. Secondly, money was lacking: after World War I the railways were almost always strapped for cash. Thirdly, and most importantly, the volume of traffic through each was too great: even St Pancras, which looked certain to close in the 1960s, is now too busy for its traffic to be comfortably absorbed by other termini.

Euston

Euston station takes its name from the eponymous square that once straddled Euston Road (part of the mid-18th-century traffic by-pass known as the New Road until 1857). Euston Square was originally far bigger than the remnant retaining the name today and included the land on which Friends' House (national headquarters of the Society of Friends – the Quakers) is built.

The square had been laid out on land belonging to the Fitzroy family, whose country seat is at Euston, Suffolk.

The station today is a place of no great interest to railway lovers: efficient but barren, it has few fans. Old Euston, however, was a fantastic agglomeration of buildings without coherent theme or pattern. Two constructions – the Arch and the Great Hall – were among the capital's finest buildings. The rest, however, were unworthy of what was once called "the most famous railway station in the world". Old Euston was terribly inefficient as a station; *The Builder* called it "a secret labyrinth" (21 April 1916).

The crowning glory of old Euston was the famous arch, sometimes (more accurately) called the Doric portico or propylaeum [2]. This was erected to celebrate the arrival in the capital of the London and Birmingham Railway, London's first main-line railway, although it was not ready for the station's opening on 20 July 1837, being completed in May the following year. The architect was Philip Hardwick. The Arch relied for effect on size. And it *was* big: 72ft 6in high. It was flanked by four pavilions or lodges, joined by elaborate iron gates decorated with the company's coat of arms (one of which is now on display at the National Railway Museum in York).

2 The famous Euston 'Arch' (1838), imposing but cluttered

PLATFORMS
2.3.4.5.6.7

The whole ensemble was built of Bramley Fall stone and cost around £35,000. A little-known fact: the Arch was hollow. Spiral staircases within the pillars led up to hideously cramped, ill-lit offices.

In 1870 the Arch was revamped and the station's name was carved on the architrave. Eleven years later, construction of railway offices destroyed the western lodge. This was the beginning of the end; the portico gradually became hemmed in by buildings, and space to appreciate its grandeur was lost.

Euston's second gem was the Great Hall, Europe's grandest waiting room [3]. This commemorated the creation of the London & North Western Railway, the largest of the pre-1923 companies. The Great Hall opened on 27 May 1849, and was designed by Philip Charles Hardwick, son of Philip. It was built on a breathtaking scale. A double staircase led up to a gallery leading to the glorious Renaissance-style shareholders' meeting room and other offices. Arches on the sides led to two booking halls, whose ceilings merged into domes similar to that on the ill-fated Coal Exchange. Plaster bas-reliefs, two to a corner, bore personifications of the principal towns served by the LNWR. These and the Britannia group above the door to the shareholders' meeting room were the work of John Thomas, who worked with Hardwick on the Great Western Hotel at Paddington

11

3   (left) The Great Hall at Euston. The LNWR Boer War memorial plaque is behind Baily's stone statue of George Stephenson

4   (below) The Euston Hotel, rear view (original 1830s buildings to left and right)

station. The work cost a fortune, at £150,000 more than the whole of King's Cross. Even so, the stinginess of the North Western undermined the grandeur of the building. The walls were of cement painted grey to simulate granite, while the columns were plaster painted to resemble red granite, the 'marble' bases being painted white. The biggest affront to Hardwick's scheme was the omission of suitable wall paintings, which left the side walls blank and unrelieved.

In front of the Arch, and blocking the view of it, was the Euston Hotel. This was a rather dull affair, partly of the 1830s by Philip Hardwick Sr [4, p 11] and with a particularly ugly 1881 addition by J McLaren [5], but it had the distinction of being the first railway hotel in the world.

Both the Arch and the Great Hall were erected without regard for passengers' convenience in reaching trains: Euston was not a sensibly designed terminus, but an assemblage of ill-fitting parts. Reconstruction was inevitable. Rebuilding was first proposed in 1900, but the LNWR balked at the cost. The LMS's 1935 plan for reconstruction of Euston would have replaced the Arch and Great Hall with a gigantic block in the restrained *art deco* style of adjacent Euston House in Eversholt Street. World War II put paid to this scheme.

After bomb damage during the war, the Great Hall was immaculately restored in 1951–3, but a decade later the whole area between Euston Road and the platforms was levelled. The Arch was pulled down by March 1962, while the Great Hall and the

5 The Euston Hotel (front view), a late Victorian traffic impediment

hotel lasted a while longer. Although strenuous efforts to save the Arch were made by private organisations including the Victorian Society, the government and British Rail were determined not to countenance preservation. However, the obliging contractor numbered the stones as they were pulled down. These have recently been located, and the Euston Arch Trust is currently campaigning for its restoration.

The present Euston station was opened in stages: the platforms were brought into use from 1966, while the main concourse building, designed by R L Moorcroft, was officially opened by the Queen on 14 October 1968.

The surviving features of old Euston are few indeed. J B Stansby's lodges on Euston Road date from 1870 and list the destinations once reached, some by rather tortuous routes, from Euston. The applied sculpture is by Joseph Pitts. The LNWR war (World War I) memorial, by Euston Road, was unveiled on 21 October 1921 by Douglas Haig. Designed by Robert Wynn Owen, it portrays typical servicemen from the navy, infantry, air force and artillery. On the windswept area in front of the modern station can be found Baron Marochetti's statue of Robert Stephenson. This was erected at the station in 1871 and originally stood between the Euston Road lodges. Two other relics of old Euston were saved. The marble statue of George Stephenson by E H Baily, formerly standing at the foot of the stairs in the Great Hall, is now at the National Railway Museum, while the carving

of Britannia and friends, also formerly in the Great Hall, is currently in storage.

Apart from the station itself there are several other important railway-related sites in the area. Euston House is a bulky 1930s 'moderne' edifice on the east side of Eversholt Street, south of Doric Way. Completed in the spring of 1934 and designed by W H Hamlyn and A V Heal, it was built as offices for the LMS Railway company. On the opposite side of the road and north of Barnby Street are the former offices of the Railway Clearing House, dating from mid-Victorian times. This organisation was set up in 1842 essentially as an inter-company accounting body to ease the difficulties of charging and invoicing for through-passenger and goods traffic. There is also the site of Richard Trevithick's experimental line of 1808. This was a simple circle of track erected in a field near the junction of Gower Street and Euston Road where the early locomotive 'Catch-me-who-can' demonstrated the possibilities of steam traction. Although it was really no more than a toy, Camden can nonetheless boast the first steam railway in London!

King's Cross

"The Cross" is one of the little-sung wonders of London's Victorian architectural heritage. Arriving from the North one is suddenly transported from a grim industrial wasteland under redevelopment into huge echoing halls of iron and glass [6, p 14] filled with noise and trains. King's Cross seems far more modern than St Pancras, perhaps because of Lewis Cubitt's functional design. Yet 150-year-old King's Cross station is London's oldest railway building and is still performing the task for which it was designed.

The King's Cross area assumed its present name in the 1820s. A short-lived memorial to King George IV, designed by the unfortunate Stephen Geary, badly executed and completed in 1835, stood for 10 years at the junction of what are now Euston Road, Gray's Inn Road and York Way. Battle Bridge, the previous name of the area, was derived from 'Bradford' (i.e. broad ford). It did not refer to a battle between the Romans and Boudicca, who is *not* buried under the station, as has sometimes been claimed.

King's Cross station was the London terminus and headquarters of the Great Northern Railway. Initially promoted as the London and York Railway, the Great Northern ran up through the East Midlands to meet the North Eastern Railway (a wealthy northern company) near Doncaster, thus forming the first link in the East Coast main line to Edinburgh. The GNR was authorised in 1846, and construction began at once. A general economic downturn meant that cash was scarce, and immediate returns were needed. The company also wanted its share of the Great Exhibition traffic.

Because of construction delays the railway at first ended at a temporary terminus (*Maiden Lane*) north of the Regent's Canal

6 King's Cross station, main arrival platform. Left centre, a water column

alongside York Way, which was known as Maiden Lane at that time. This opened on 7 August 1850 and was used until the permanent station was ready. The temporary station was then integrated into the company's goods depot and used as a potato market. Some of the physical structure of the temporary station remained *in situ* until 1988, when it was demolished.

Cubitt's station opened on 14 October 1852. Two huge semicircular arched roofs span the platform area. The ribs of these were originally made of laminated timber to reduce construction time and save money, but these showed signs of failing and were replaced with iron (the eastern span in 1866–7, the western in 1886–7). The covered area is 800 ft long, 210 ft wide and 72 ft high. The frontage on Euston Road [7] is of plain brick pierced by lunettes echoing the line of the roof profile, with arcades at ground level for access. Perched on top, rather incongruously, is an Italianate clock tower. This houses a timepiece exhibited in the Great Exhibition of 1851, the chimes of which have recently been brought back into use. A range of offices with Venetian styling is located to the west, while a cab road (no longer used as such) is to the east.

Before the demise of steam locomotives King's Cross suffered severe working difficulties, essentially because there was a lack of space between the ends of the platforms and the Gasworks Tunnels (the bores immediately north of the station, taking their name from the nearby works of the former Imperial Gas Light and Coke Company). Another difficulty was that traffic outgrew the volume available inside the main train shed. This problem was partly solved by adding extra platforms inside the shed: originally there were only two platforms, for departures on the west and for arrivals next to the cab road opposite. However, it was soon necessary to add extra platforms still further west. These form the

15

7 King's Cross station, main frontage (Lewis Cubitt, 1850)

suburban station, which has a complicated history, but the bulk of the fabric currently in use dates from 1895. There were further extensions to this as well as an additional platform on York Way known as *King's Cross York Road.* This platform was often treated as an entirely separate station, and was in use from 1866 to 1977 for trains running to Moorgate and elsewhere, via the City Widened Lines (see description under Circle Line on p 36).

The station has been substantially extended since it opened. One of the earliest alterations was a range of offices erected over the cab road (the difference in brick coloration is revealing here), while the most obvious was the filling in of the space between the façade of the station and Euston Road. This area, once known as the 'Indian Village', was created by the westward diversion of Pancras Road in 1871. The current appearance of this area dates from 1973. The original line of the road accounts for the curved profile of the Great Northern Hotel (also designed by Cubitt and erected at the same time as the station).

Perhaps the most fundamental alteration to the original fabric resulted from bomb damage. Early on the morning of 11 May 1941 a heavy explosive bomb, probably a single 500-kg bomb, made a direct hit on the western range of offices, from which a considerable chunk was bitten out. Only temporary repairs were ever made and the damage is obvious today. The blast also brought down four of the arched ribs. These were replaced after the war; an observant eye can detect the difference in pattern.

Essentially, the station is in much the same condition as when it opened, though redevelopment was seriously considered in the 1940s. A model prepared for the LNER showed a new office block fronting the sheds and an irregularly shaped two-storey structure fronting Euston Road. Both were to be in the plain 'moderne' style used, for instance, at Stratford in East London. Shortage of money and nationalisation of the railways caused these plans to be abandoned.

St Pancras

The station takes its name from St Pancras Old Church, whose graveyard was partly removed for the building of the immediate approaches to the station. Saint Pancras was a 4th-century boy martyr in Ancient Rome (he is *not* the patron saint of train spotters, as has sometimes been alleged).

Many people refer to the magnificent neo-gothic masterpiece of George Gilbert Scott as St Pancras station, whereas it is of course the station *hotel*, originally the Midland Grand Hotel, and now after many years of disuse called St Pancras Chambers. It is almost certainly the most famous railway building in Britain (see pp 18–19). The station proper, designed by William Barlow, lies behind, the platforms spanned by an immense curved roof, also world-famous for the extent of its span.

The station was opened on 1 October 1868 as the London

terminus of the Midland Railway. This company, based in Derby, had for many years been seeking access to London. From 1844 to 1857 it had used Euston via a connection at Rugby with the LNWR. After this an agreement was made with the GNR. Both arrangements had financial and operational disadvantages, and in 1862 the decision was made to make an independent entry into the capital.

The Midland (like the Great Central later in the century) was an intruder, seeking to lure traffic away from established lines. This it did by providing better terminal facilities – the Midland Grand Hotel was one of the most up-to-date and sumptuous of its day – and by advertisement on a grand scale: St Pancras can be read as an enormous billboard proclaiming the merits not only of the railway company but of the railway's catchment area and its companies. Thus each of the huge ribs of the train shed still proudly bear the legend "manufactured by the Butterley Company, Derbyshire 1867".

This roof is vast – 690 ft long, with a span of 240 ft – and was the biggest of its type in the world when completed [8]. It was later surpassed in width (the real technical achievement) by the sheds at several American stations: Broad Street, Philadelphia (the widest ever at 300 ft, burnt out in 1923, later demolished); Reading Terminal, Philadelphia (still existing but out of railway use); and

8   St Pancras station interior: the largest single-span train shed in the world

Pennsylvania Railroad depot, Jersey City (demolished). As far as can be ascertained it is at present the widest train shed in the world. The engineer, William Henry Barlow, reputedly introduced the slight peak to the train shed to reduce wind resistance, although doubtless stylistic considerations were also a factor.

The most original feature of the station is not usually visible. The platforms are well above ground level because the tracks must cross the Regent's Canal just to the north of the station, and the resulting space below the station was originally utilised to store beer from Burton-on-Trent. The dark catacombs between the sturdy cast-iron columns supporting the platforms and tracks above are now in use as workshops as well as for car parking, and are well worth a look.

One level further down is the railway tunnel connecting King's Cross Thameslink station with Kentish Town, which runs under the station at this point. The isolated St Pancras Tunnel signal box (in use 1889 to 1958) was located here. Access was via a spiral staircase, which debouched onto the east side of Midland Road (see reference to 'King's Cross tunnel' on p 21).

The **hotel** was a later addition and was designed independently of Barlow's roof, as can be inferred by the less than perfect join between the two. The design was original [9] and *not* adapted from Scott's plan for a neo-Gothic Foreign Office. Scott's first plan for the hotel included an additional floor which was never built. The main phase of construction began in 1869, and the hotel received its first guests on 5 May 1873, but the curved west wing was not finished until 1876. The hotel closed on 19 April 1935, parts of it afterwards being used as offices. Present visitors can on certain days view the magnificent restored main staircase and other features. The booking hall, originally with a hammerbeam style roof, is stylistically part of the hotel. Although extensively altered, most recently in 1988, this is still one of the station's most interesting features. The corbels on the north side featuring stylised railway employees are perhaps the best work here.

The station bears scars from both world wars. A bomb exploded near the cab approach to the main booking office on the night of 17 February 1917, killing several people. Pockmarks on the granite arches still bear witness to this attack. During World War II the station was again badly hit. Several accounts attribute the loss of Scott's booking-office roof to the Blitz, but this is not true. A mediocre flat roof had been installed sometime earlier, and it was this, not the Victorian original, that collapsed.

Two other incidents are worthy of notice. During the night of 15/16 October 1940 a parachute mine fell on the station, becoming caught on signals at the end of the westernmost island platform.

9   The Midland Grand Hotel (c.1950) by George Gilbert Scott, opened 1873

After two hours it exploded, destroying most of the glass in the roof. The stumpy brick tower that terminates the side wall of the train shed was also damaged (the brighter colour of replacement brickwork can be clearly seen). Probably the most photographed station incident of the war occurred at St Pancras on the night of 10/11 May 1941. At the head of platform 3 a huge crater was opened up which reached down to the underground line beneath. The damage was virtually made good within a week.

Despite its fame, St Pancras was never the heart of the Midland's system, which remained at Derby. Even today the station has a different atmosphere from Euston and King's Cross: great railway journeys do not start here. It is purely the London terminus of an essentially provincial line. As such, it has several times been under threat of closure; but it has survived and is projected to become a terminus for trains from the Continent via the Channel Tunnel. For this reason St Pancras station is owned by London & Continental Railways (all other stations being owned by Railtrack).

Annotated bibliography for Section 2

General: *Of the many printed sources for the termini, those mentioned below are the ones I have found particularly useful or interesting. Jackson's book is a general guide to all London's termini that has never been bettered (a more recent edition has just been released). Betjeman & Gay contains an interesting commentary and atmospheric photographs. Kellett's work is especially useful in explaining the role of land ownership in railway development and refers in detail to Camden's 'big three'. The* Railway Magazine *articles in the 'notable railway stations' series are lengthy profiles of the big stations during the height of their importance and contain valuable maps, contemporary descriptions and atmospheric photographs – that for Euston of 1914 is similar.*

1. Euston: *The 1849 article on "Euston Square" (the station was unofficially known as* Euston Square *during its early existence) has a very detailed description of the Great Hall. The 1968 booklet is useful for its description of the new station and its construction. The 1968 article on Euston, despite its title, is an account of the 1935 rebuilding plan.*

2. King's Cross: *Hunter & Thorne is a historical and archaeological survey of the King's Cross area as a whole, but contains valuable information on the passenger station and hotel (it also covers St Pancras). The 1925 item on King's Cross relates mostly to the partial rebuilding of the suburban station in that year. Robert Leon in* Camden History Review 19 *gives the history of the King's Cross itself. The 1952 article by C A Johns is an excellent summary. The* London Railway Record *includes details on the temporary Maiden Lane station, which is also covered in Hunter & Thorne.*

3. St Pancras: *Jack Simmons's book is definitely the best station history produced. The 1936 article on "King's Cross Tunnel" is actually* *about the Midland tunnel under St Pancras. Charles E Lee's centenary article on St Pancras for the* Railway Magazine *is a classic modern piece.*

Books
General

Alan A Jackson, *London's termini* (David & Charles, 1969)

John R Kellett, *The impact of railways on Victorian cities* (Routledge & Kegan Paul, 1969)

John Betjeman & John Gay, *London's historic railway stations* (John Murray, 1972)

KA Scholey, *London's Railways* (Tempus, 1999)

Euston

The new Euston station 1968 (British Rail, 1968)

King's Cross

M Hunter & R Thorne (eds) *Change at King's Cross* (Historical Publications, 1990)

Chris Hawkins *The great British railway station: King's Cross* (Irwell Press, 1990)

St Pancras

Jack Simmons *St Pancras station* (George Allen & Unwin, 1968)

M Hunter & R Thorne (eds) *Change at King's Cross* (Historical Publications, 1990)

Articles
Euston

"New station…Euston Square" in *Illustrated London News*, 2 June 1849

"The most famous railway station in the world… Euston…" in *Railway Magazine*, May 1914

"Euston House" in *LMS Railway Magazine*, Mar 1934

"Euston nears completion" in *Railway Magazine*, Oct 1968

"The Railway Clearing House" in *Backtrack*, July/ Aug 1993

"Recollections of Euston and St Pancras" in *Camden History Review* 19 (1995)

King's Cross

"Notable railway stations: King's Cross" in *Railway Magazine*, Aug 1914

"Recent developments at King's Cross" in *Railway Magazine*, Mar 1925

"King's Cross station: a rebuilding scheme" in *The Builder*, 22 Feb 1946

"One hundred years at King's Cross" in *Railway Magazine*, Oct & Nov 1952

"The man who made King's Cross" in *Camden History Review* 17 (1992)

"Maiden Lane station" in *The London Railway Record*, July 1996

St Pancras

"Notable railway stations: 19. St Pancras" in *Railway Magazine*, June 1902

"King's Cross tunnel" in *LMS Railway Magazine*, Aug 1936

"St Pancras station, 1868-1968" in *Railway Magazine*, Sept & Oct 1968

"Recollections of Euston and St Pancras" in *Camden History Review* 19 (1995)

3 The surface lines

The configuration of the surface lines – generally running east to west and parallel to one another – is largely a product of the geography of the area. To the north of the borough the land rises steeply up to the "Northern Heights" (Highgate and Hampstead). This was a great barrier to railway building: tunnelling was expensive and was therefore avoided whenever possible. Since it was impossible because of gradients to go over, and too expensive to go under, the railways had to go round. The LNWR and Midland curved round to the west, the GNR went east. The same factors influenced the siting of the North London and Hampstead Junction Railways.

The layout of the area's railways also reflects the shape of London at the time they were built – built-up areas had to be avoided if the cost of land purchase were to be minimised. Thus the pattern for the approaches to the termini was, basically, to creep round the edge of the suburban belt and then turn sharply in. This was true also for the circular railways, the North London & the Gospel Oak-Barking lines. Indeed, when the Hampstead Junction line was constructed it ran almost entirely through fields, where the little that had been built was of poor quality and occupied by the poorest class.

As with the major termini, land ownership was important. Districts that became particularly loaded with railways (Finchley Road, and to the west of Camden Town) had few owners. The law agent for the London & Birmingham (Euston line) said shortly after the opening of the line "All the land we bought in [central] London was entirely the property of Lord Southampton, and then we got into Eton College property. Up to the river Brent, 6 miles from London, there were scarcely more than six or eight proprietors" (quoted on p 246 of Kellett). As explained in the Introduction (p 6), railway owners always preferred to deal with few landowners because of the speed and simplicity in negotiations.

It is important to recognise that in no sense were the railways in the borough built for the local inhabitants. The main-line railways were merely passing through from their northern heartlands, while the cross-London routes (North London and Tottenham & Hampstead) originated as 'long sidings' from the main lines to the docks (those at Poplar and at Tilbury respectively). The Hampstead Junction Railway was built essentially as a cut-off to avoid the LNWR's busy Camden goods yard, and again was primarily a goods line. Because they were merely traversing the area on the way to other places, little attention was given to passenger accommodation, which was therefore often Spartan in the extreme. In the case of the North London Line this statement must be modified somewhat, as the meagre passenger services that were originally provided proved extremely popular and very profitable, especially after the opening of the line to the City in 1865. A series of large, even magnificent, stations for the use of suburban commuters was therefore built.

Main lines
North Western main line
The first railway line in Camden was the London & Birmingham Railway. This was London's first main line and in many ways is the most important, as it links the capital with Britain's three largest provincial cities – Birmingham, Liverpool and Manchester. The L&B opened from Euston to Boxmoor (now Hemel Hempstead station in Hertfordshire) on 20 July 1837, being completed through to the 'second city' the following year. Initially the line was planned to begin near Camden Town at the site of the later goods depot and engine sheds (see pp 44–45 in section 5 for further details). In 1846 the L&B amalgamated with several other companies to become the London & North Western Railway, the largest of the pre-1914 companies. For many years afterwards the development of this line and its surroundings was retarded by the LNWR's conservative policies.

The line was originally double-track, but a third line for goods use was laid north of Primrose Hill

10   Primrose Hill tunnel: the magnificent south portal as originally built

tunnel [10 p23] in 1859. A second Primrose Hill tunnel was opened in 1879, after which the line was four-tracked over its entire length. In the first quarter of the twentieth century a separate line for local trains to Watford was built parallel to the main lines. The "New Line" was designed for four-rail DC electric trains and opened in stages from 1912. The section within Camden (Euston to Queen's Park) opened on 10 July 1922. The major work here was an elaborate system of burrowing junctions at Chalk Farm. The slow lines for outer suburban services (e.g. to Milton Keynes), together with the fast lines, were electrified in 1966. (Much material of interest on this line can be found in Section 8 of Edwin Course's *London Railways*, see p 33 for details.)

Stations

Chalk Farm was known as *Camden* from 1844 to 1866, and *Camden (Chalk Farm)* from 1866 to 1876. As early as 1844 there was a ticket platform (a stop enabling tickets to be checked) here, and a public station followed on 1 November 1851. This was re-sited the following year. Rebuilding in 1872 provided a footbridge link to the adjacent North London station (later known as Primrose Hill), the booking office of which served both lines. The station closed through wartime economy measures on 10 May 1915. No traces of the old LNWR platforms remain today.

South Hampstead opened as *Loudoun Road* [11] on 2 June 1879. Temporarily closed from 1917 to 1922 it reopened with the present

11   Loudoun Road LNWR station, once a pretty little affair

name but was served by New Line electric trains only (the site of the old main-line platforms can easily be traced). The street building, a charming wooden affair with attractive chimney-stacks, has been demolished.

Kilburn High Road was plain *Kilburn* when it opened around 1852. Its platforms in c.1905 are shown in [12]. The station became *Kilburn & Maida Vale* in 1879, when it received a new street building on the bridge. This was originally dominated by a large glass-and-iron porch, which was a feature of many LNWR stations. The porch was removed during World War II, the rest of the bridge-building lasting another 20 years or so. An earlier building, probably dating from the 1840s, alongside the London-bound

platform and fronting Belsize Road, still exists and is in use as a Lebanese restaurant. Like South Hampstead, Kilburn was temporarily closed during the First World War, reopening with platforms served only by the new electric trains. Here, however, the widening was on the south side of the formation, so that the present platforms formerly served the slow service operating on the main line. The station received its current name in 1923.

Midland main line
The Midland Railway ploughed its way through the borough in the mid-1860s, the first sod on the new line being turned in July 1865 near Kentish Town Road. In this area was the contractor's main yard, with extensive workshops and office, and

12 Kilburn High Road station in action before World War I

a claypit where bricks for the railway works were extracted and fired. The line opened for goods on 9 September 1867; for local services to Moorgate (via an underground tunnel under St Pancras station and the City Widened Lines – see p 36) on 13 July 1868; and for long-distance traffic from the North and the Midlands into St Pancras on 1 October. The line consisted originally of four tracks south of Welsh Harp Junction (south of Hendon), although these were squeezed through one bore of Belsize Tunnel under Haverstock Hill. A second Belsize Tunnel was added in 1884. In 1895 a new goods line was laid. The old Midland main line was electrified using overhead wires in 1982.

Stations

The Midland route had five stations in the borough, but only two of those are still open. The Midland's inner suburban service was never much favoured by the company, which preferred to rely on its lucrative long-distance goods and coal trade. With no established clientèle these stations easily fell victim to the fierce bus, tram and Tube competition.

Camden Road was the first station out of St Pancras and opened on 13 July 1868. The single-storeyed street building, typical of those on the Inner London stretch of the Midland, was a substantial but dull brick affair, characterised by a low, pitched roof with overhanging eaves. It was located on the north side of Camden Road almost on the corner of Sandall Road. The station closed on 1 January 1916 as the result of wartime economies. The street building has been replaced by a petrol station and there is little to be seen at rail level. **Kentish Town** also dated from the opening of the line in 1868. The station was rebuilt in Edwardian times (in connection with widening) and again around 1981, when a joint booking hall with the Underground was opened. The ornate metal structure in the roadway outside was once part of Elstree station and was re-erected here after the 1980s rebuilding.

Haverstock Hill [13], like Camden Road, was in use from 1868 until 1916. The street building, located on the corner of Lismore Circus and what is now New Rochford Street, had the ornate bargeboards more commonly seen on the Midland's country stations: clearly, a special effort was made for what was then a better-quality neighbourhood. The building was demolished after a fire in the 1960s, although by that time the platform structures (dating from 1884) had long been gone. (A detailed account of the history of this station can be found in the April 1996 issue of The London Railway Record.)

Finchley Road was again an original station on the line. The platforms were re-sited in 1884 (the conversion of the first Belsize tunnel to goods use having rendered the earlier pair redundant), but the booking-office building of 1868 remained in use until the station closed on 11 July 1927. Located below street level, this was a standard structure resembling that at Camden Road, but with an upper storey. It was demolished in the 1960s. The small crescent of shops and the entrance arch bearing the station name were erected in Edwardian times, and are still to be found on the west side of Finchley Road, where the Midland line passes under. There is no connection with the present Finchley Road *Tube* station, which lies 100 yards further south, on the same side of the Finchley Road. (A detailed history of this station can be found in the July 1997 issue of *The London Railway Record*.)

West Hampstead opened on 1 March 1871 and was known as *West End* (the name of the village which preceded West Hampstead) until 1905. The station was largely rebuilt in 1903; the rebuilt booking-office building on the bridge was in the reddish-brown terracotta favoured by the company at this time. It was demolished in 1981. A rare prefabricated platform building of 1945 survived the rebuilding. Plans are currently afoot to reconstruct the station as an interchange site.

Great Northern Railway

The immediate approach to King's Cross, including the three Gasworks Tunnels (the easternmost of which is out of use) under the Regent's Canal, was opened in 1852. As explained in the section on King's Cross, the main line to the north opened two years earlier from the temporary station in Maiden Lane. This passes north-east under York Way (and out of the borough), then north to Finsbury Park.

13 Haverstock Hill station – brick with gingerbread details

Great Central Railway

Running in from the west parallel to the Metropolitan line as far as West Hampstead and then forking off south to Marylebone is the former Great Central Railway main line (opened 1898 for coal traffic, full goods and passenger services in 1899). This was built as the London extension of the provincial Manchester, Sheffield and Lincolnshire Railway. The MS&L hoped to cash in on the London trade, and with this in mind adopted the name Great Central. The line is in use for local traffic to Aylesbury and Banbury and, after a lengthy absence, long-distance traffic has been restored in the form of a service to Birmingham via Leamington Spa.

East–West lines

The main east–west route is the North London Line (North Woolwich to Richmond). This is a fusion of several lines, each with its own identity and history. Two railways are associated with the part of the North London line in Camden: the North London Railway proper and the Hampstead Junction Railway. Branching off from the North London is the Gospel Oak–Barking line. Silverlink Metro currently operates passenger services on both lines.

North London Railway

The original North London Railway ran from the LNWR main line near Chalk Farm to the Docks at Poplar. Until 1853 it was known as the East & West India Dock and Birmingham Junction Railway. Before this it was referred to as "The Camden Town Railway" (e.g. in the *Illustrated London News* of 15 November 1851) and can thus be claimed as Camden's own, although only a short stretch lies in the borough. The section from Islington (now Highbury & Islington)

14 Camden Town (now Camden Road) NLR station in c.1905. Note the advertised time to the City

to Camden Town opened on 7 December 1850. A further extension to the LNWR opened on 9 June 1851. In 1871 the line was widened east of Camden Road (including the station) to give four tracks. The route from Broad Street to Richmond was electrified in 1916, and from Camden Road Junction (west of the station) to Queen's Park in 1922. The North London became part of the LNWR in 1922. The section of the line west of Camden Road Junction closed to passengers on 22 September 1992 but is still open for goods.

Stations

Maiden Lane was opened on 1 July 1887 and closed on 1 January 1917. The nondescript booking-office building of two storeys, located on the west side of York Way just north of the North London Line bridge, was demolished in the 1970s.

Camden Road (*Camden Town* until 1950) is the most impressive of the small stations in the borough. The street building [14], designed by Edwin Henry Horne, the North London's architect, dates from when the station was opened on 5 December 1870. It is a fine example of the company's 'Italianate' style and features the characteristic cement panels bearing the company and station names at cornice level. An earlier station, dating from 1850, was located some way to the east. Perhaps worthy of note was the signal box erected in 1860 just to the west of the present station, controlling access to and from the Hampstead Junction line. According to the *LMSR Magazine* of 1929 this was the first interlocking signal box in the world! (Interlocking is a vital safety feature which allows signals to be worked only in unison with the points of a junction.)

Primrose Hill opened on 9 June 1851 as *Hampstead Road*. The

29

15   The grandiose entrance to Chalk Farm (later Primrose Hill) station in early British Rail days

station was re-sited just four years later, renamed *Chalk Farm* in 1862 and again rebuilt in 1871. The 1871 station [p 29] was designed by Henry Woodhouse of the LNWR Engineer's Office in Stafford. In 1950 the station became *Primrose Hill* and the street building was reconstructed. This was once a busy little station, but the adjacent Tube station (named *Chalk Farm*) took away most of its traffic, and Primrose Hill closed on 22 September 1992. The street building, on the south-east side of Regent's Park Road, north of Gloucester Avenue, has been extensively altered and is now in use as an antiques shop. The island platform with its buildings remains *in situ*.

Hampstead Junction Railway

The other part of the North London line in Camden was officially called the North and South Western, Hampstead and City Junction Railway, but this was (understandably!) shortened to the Hampstead Junction Railway. This opened from Camden Road Junction – west of Camden Road station – to Willesden on 2 January 1860. Originally an independent company, after a few years the HJR was taken over by the LNWR. The line was electrified in 1916. The HJR was in the odd position of being owned by one company (the North Western) but with train services almost exclusively supplied by another (the North London).

Stations

Kentish Town West opened on 1 April 1867 and was plain Kentish Town until 1923. The street buildings,

located either side of the bridge over Prince of Wales Road, seem to be partly original, although they have recently been extensively altered. The platforms were made of wood and have been totally destroyed by fire twice – on 26 August 1872 and again on 18 April 1971, almost 100 years apart. After the second fire the station was closed for 10 years before being rebuilt with GLC funds. The reopening ceremony was performed by Ken Livingstone (now Mayor of London).

Gospel Oak station, on the north side of Mansfield Road just before it meets Gordon House Road, was an original stop of 1860 and was known until 1867 as *Kentish Town*. The station was entirely reconstructed in a modernistic but plain style in 1953.

Hampstead Heath, on South End Road by South End Green, was an original station on the line. The exterior was originally a single-storey brick building with austere decoration, but was replaced in 1968 by the current one (in the style known as 'modern public convenience'). The platform buildings were replaced in 1953 with cantilevered concrete canopies similar to those at Gospel Oak. These did not age well, and the current traditional platform awnings date from 1996. The station was the site of a terrible accident on 19 April 1892 when six people were crushed to death.

Finchley Road & Frognal [16, 17] (the third station on the west side of the Finchley Road bearing similar names!) was opened at the same time as *Hampstead Heath* and

16 Finchley Road & Frognal station, typical unattractive HJR station

17 Waiting for trains at Finchley Road & Frognal station (busy goods yard to the right)

originally much resembled it. The current exterior dates from 1969–70, when all platform buildings were removed.

32   **West Hampstead** (originally *West End Lane*) opened on 1 March 1888. This station retains its original brick, LNWR-style street building although the platform buildings were removed during the North London tidying campaign of 1968–70. It is the middle one of another triplet of stations even closer together than those on the Finchley Road.

Gospel Oak–Barking line

The Gospel Oak to Barking line is a strange backwater of a railway, known to few living along its route, but with a regular and apparently well-used service. Only a small part lies in Camden. The line started life as the Tottenham & Hampstead Junction Railway, which like the Hampstead Junction Railway was an independent concern. This opened between Tottenham North Junction (south of Tottenham Hale station) and Highgate Road on 21 July 1868. The Midland Railway opened a connecting line from Kentish Town to Highgate Road (the South Curve) on 3 January 1870. Henceforth the Midland provided the main passenger service over the line by means of trains to Moorgate; this service was later cut short to terminate at Kentish Town. The Midland had two other connecting lines to the T&HJR: from erstwhile Carlton Road to Camden Road Junction, opened in 1883 (exclusively for goods); and a further stretch skirting the locomotive depot dating from 1900 (latterly carrying

the main passenger service). The short stretch from Highgate Road (High Level) to Gospel Oak was opened on 4 June 1888, thus fulfilling the Hampstead Junction part of the railway's title after nearly 20 years! There was, however, no permanent rail connection to the Hampstead Junction line until 1940. In 1902 the T&HJR became the shared property of the Great Eastern and Midland Railways and the "Junction" in the title became "Joint". In 1964 the South Curve was closed. In 1981 the 1900 Midland line was lifted, but the 1883 connection to the north remains in active use for goods traffic.

Stations

There were three stations on the T&HJR and associated lines in Camden.

Gospel Oak, now the western passenger terminus, is a recent addition, opening on 5 January 1981, but it stands on the site of a station in regular use between 4 June 1888 and 6 September 1926. This is the third station on the same site, as platforms were partially constructed in 1868 but never used.

Highgate Road (High Level) opened on 21 July 1868 and closed on 1 October 1915. It was entered through an arch (still extant) under the Highgate Road bridge.

Highgate Road (Low Level) station was owned by the Midland Railway. It opened on 17 December 1900, closed on 1 March 1918, and was located in a cutting immediately south of the High Level. There are very few physical traces.

Annotated bibliography for section 3

General: *Borley's work in particular is an indispensable guide to dates of opening and closure. Connor and Halford give short sketches of closed stations. Michael Alpert's article in the Camden History Review in 1979 is a good area study of a locality served by the Midland, Hampstead Junction and Metropolitan Railways.*

1. Main lines: *There are few really useful works on the main lines; material relating to these has been pieced together from various sources. Section eight of Course's work is a very useful history of the Euston to Willesden Junction section of the old LNWR.*

2. East–West lines: *Connor's books are predominantly pictorial but are the best guide to the North London and Tottenham Joint lines. Material on the old North London Railway is abundant but the 1898 "illustrated interview" is a little-known piece, of exceptional period value, which gives useful contemporary information on one of London's most popular local railways at the height of its use. The 1929 article refers to the Camden Road signal box mentioned in the text. Ms Cedar's thesis particularly focuses on the impact of the Hampstead Junction line. The author's own article on the HJR appeared in* Backtrack *in October 2000 and is derived principally from the minute books of that company.*

Books

General

H V Borley, *Chronology of London Railways* (Railway & Canal Historical Society, 1982)

J E Connor & B L Halford, *Forgotten stations of Greater London* (Connor & Butler, 1991)

John R Kellett, *The impact of railways on Victorian cities* (Routledge & Kegan Paul, 1969)

K A Scholey, *London's Railways* (Tempus, 1999)

Main lines (LNWR, Midland)

F Atkinson & B Adams, *London's North Western Electric* (Electric Railway Society, 1962)

Edwin Course, *London Railways* (BT Batsford, 1962)

Geoff Goslin, *The London extension of the Midland Railway* (Irwell Press, 1994)

J B Radford, *Midland Line memories* (Midas, 1983)

East–West lines (North London, Hampstead Junction, Gospel Oak–Barking)

J E Connor, *Broad Street to Primrose Hill* (Connor & Butler, 1996)

Vic Mitchell & Keith Smith, *North London Line* (Middleton Press, 1997)

Valerie Cedar, *Urban development in Camden...1840-90* (unpublished thesis, c. 1978)

J E Connor, *The Tottenham Joint Lines* (Connor & Butler, 1993)

Articles

General

"West Hampstead's railway invasion" in *Camden History Review 7* (1979).

Main lines (LNWR, Midland)

"Finchley Road remembered" in *The*

Workmen enjoying a celebration dinner at the Gower Street
(present Euston Square) Underground station, 1862. See p 37

4 The Underground lines

The local businesses that later became the London Underground started, like the main lines, as private companies. The first, the Metropolitan Railway, originated as a link between the three main-line termini (Paddington, Euston and King's Cross) and the City of London (Farringdon), but soon spread into suburbia and beyond. The 'Met' ran large-profile (initially steam) trains in shallow tunnels in the central area, but elsewhere functioned as an ordinary railway. Really efficient transport in inner London had to await the advent of the tubes – all-electric, deep-bored tunnels – in the 1890s. The genesis of today's underground system lies in a trio of lines (Bakerloo, Piccadilly and Hampstead) known as Yerkes' Tubes, after their American backer Charles Yerkes. These had a common architectural policy as well as interchangeable rolling stock and a common fares system. By 1914 most of the tubes had been taken over by a company referred to as the Underground group, an outgrowth of the Yerkes organisation. The Underground group and the Metropolitan survived the Grouping mentioned in section 1, only to be combined as London Transport under local (later, national) government control in 1933.

Several London Underground lines serve the Borough of Camden. These are of two types: the main-line-sized subsurface lines (Metropolitan and Circle) dating from the 19th century; and the small-profile deep tubes (Central, Piccadilly, Northern, Victoria and Jubilee lines) built in the last 100 years. The former used steam traction until Edwardian times, while the latter have been electric from the start.

Initially, both types of underground line had to be fitted into existing street patterns. The original Metropolitan Railway (now part of the Circle Line) for reasons of cost used tunnels under roadways, built by the so-called cut-and-cover method, alternating with brick-walled cuttings hidden at the back of buildings. The 'extension line' (the current Metropolitan Line north of Baker Street) came to the surface near Finchley Road and in its outer suburban area, a small part of which is relevant here, functioned in the same way as an ordinary railway, i.e. with embankments and earth cuttings.

The Tube lines were also constrained by cost factors. Until World War II tubes had to be hollowed out along configurations corresponding to surface features, mainly to avert the possibility of lawsuits stemming from vibration damage to buildings. Thus, the early Tube lines mostly follow the line of streets.

As the purpose of the original Metropolitan Railway was to link Paddington to Farringdon, it was not influenced by the needs of what became the Borough of Camden. However, when the 'Met' later spread its wings north from Baker Street, entering the old borough of Hampstead at Swiss Cottage, it had a considerable effect on the development of part of Camden, namely West Hampstead.

In contrast to the main-line and suburban railways, Tube lines *were* built with local inhabitants in mind – or more precisely, the profits to be had in carrying these local inhabitants around. Tube trains were essentially a response to increasing congestion in the streets. Tube lines were amply provided with stations – indeed, as it turned out, too abundantly. As the lines were extended, the many stops at intermediate stations like poorly frequented South Kentish Town proved a waste of time. The obvious solution – to build 'express lines' as in New York City – was never adopted, although the large underground bunkers built during World War II beneath Goodge Street, Camden Town, Belsize Park and Chancery Lane stations (to name only those within Camden) were intended eventually to be linked together to form such high-speed lines. The project failed through lack of funds.

One more underground railway needs to be mentioned: the Post Office Railway, which connected several major stations to postal sorting depots. The line was never intended to be used by passengers, only for the transport of mail, and has always been under remote automatic control, with no drivers. The section within the borough includes the West Central District

Post Office (off High Holborn) and has been in use since 1928. An experimental predecessor, the Pneumatic Dispatch Company, was active in the 1860s and early 1870s. Two lines ran into Euston – from the North West District Office (on what is now the Crowndale Centre site) off Eversholt Street, and from the General Post Office in St Martin's-le-Grand under High Holborn and up Tottenham Court Road. Built by an independent company, the line suffered technical problems, and was never adopted by the Post Office.

The sub-surface lines

Circle Line

The original Metropolitan Railway between Paddington and Farringdon opened on 10 January 1863. This stretch became part of the "Inner Circle", the modern Circle Line. Circle services were provided jointly with the District Line, although the Metropolitan continued to own this part of the line. For the first 40 years the Circle service used steam engines. These were fitted with a mechanism to remove the smoke, but the tunnels were still thick with sulphurous fumes. The Circle was electrified on the fourth-rail principle in 1905, but goods traffic used steam traction into the 1960s. The 'City Widened Lines', although owned by the Metropolitan, were constructed to enable Midland and Great Northern trains to run directly into the City and consist of a double-track line alongside the Circle from King's Cross to Moorgate. The separate tracks were brought into use in stages between 1866 and

1868. Link lines ran from north of King's Cross and St Pancras to join the Circle Line formation immediately west of the current Thameslink station. Only the old Midland link (officially the St Pancras branch) is currently in use as part of the Thameslink line. The steeply graded connections to the former Great Northern were closed in 1977. (The complicated history of the subsurface lines at King's Cross is told in the article "Railway connections at King's Cross"– see p 43 for details.)

Stations

King's Cross Circle Line station was opened on 14 March 1941 and inside resembles the spacious stations of the Moscow Metro. In this case, however, the layout is accidental – the large central 'concourse' is the old running line tunnel while the eastbound line uses a previously disused tunnel. Access is from a subway.

King's Cross Thameslink is on the site of the original Metropolitan King's Cross station of 1863. This was a magnificent affair with a large arched roof similar to those surviving on the western part of the Circle Line. The station was rebuilt in 1911 when the overall roof was demolished. Circle Line trains ceased to call in 1941, and the former (1911) street building [18] is now in use as shops. The platforms currently in use were opened on 17 January 1868 for the use of City Widened Lines trains, although these were out of use between 1979 and the time (1988) at which the station was again largely rebuilt.

Euston Square was one of the original stations on the line, but was originally – and more appropriately - called *Gower Street*. The platforms are located in the double-track tunnel under Euston Road. The original street buildings were single-storey in an Italianate style. These were rebuilt around 1909, when the station received its current name, again in 1931 and in the 1960s. Access today is from a subway under Euston Road.

37

18   King's Cross Circle Line entrance, 1910. Shops now occupy the booking office

Metropolitan Line

The Metropolitan Line north of Baker Street originated as a branch line to Swiss Cottage which opened on 13 April 1868. This was run by a subsidiary company, the Baker Street & St John's Wood, which was finally absorbed by the Metropolitan in 1883. From the late 1870s the Metropolitan built to the north, invading the territory of the North Western and Midland companies. This was a rather cunning manoeuvre on the part of Sir Edward Watkin, Chairman of the Metropolitan. He sought to use the Metropolitan as a stepping stone in his dream of a through route from the North to the continent, via the Manchester, Sheffield & Lincolnshire (later Great Central) and South Eastern Railways, and a projected Channel tunnel, all of which he was heavily involved in.

In the event such a connection could not be realised and the Watkin empire fell apart. The 'extension' line, as the railway north of Baker Street was known, opened as far as West Hampstead on 30 June 1879 and went on to Willesden on 24 November in the same year. The inner section has been partly taken over by the Jubilee Line (see later).

Stations

Swiss Cottage was in use between 13 April 1868 and 18 August 1940. The original street building [19], which resembled contemporary stations on the District Line such as Bayswater, was rebuilt in 1929 to the designs of C W Clark. This edifice on the west side of Finchley Road, featuring an arcade of shops, was used as an additional entrance to the nearby Bakerloo (now Jubilee) station after closure but was demolished for

19   Swiss Cottage (Metropolitan Line) station exterior c.1905, long demolished

road widening in the late 1960s. There are some traces at platform level.

Finchley Road opened on 30 June 1879. The original street building [20] was replaced in 1913–14 by one designed by F Sherrin, which survives today, though altered in 1939 when the layout of the platforms was also changed. Metropolitan and Jubilee Line trains serve the station now.

West Hampstead opened at the same time as Finchley Road. The station, including the booking office building, was largely reconstructed in 1898 in connection with the Great Central Railway's London extension. Most of the platform buildings and the interior of the street building date from 1938. Metropolitan Line trains have not stopped here since 1939, but the Jubilee Line continues to do so.

The Tube lines

Central Line

Although the Central London Railway (CLR, the core of today's Central Line) was not the first Tube railway, it was the first to be successful, imprinting itself on the public mind as the 'Tuppenny Tube' (because of the flat fare of two old pence). Public service began on 30 July 1900, when all Camden stations on the Central Line except Holborn were opened.

Stations

Chancery Lane was a standard CLR station. Platforms had white tiling. The street building was clad in 'biscuit' coloured stone, mostly functional in style but with some baroque features (architect Henry Measures). Upper floors in red brick, designed by Delissa Joseph, were added later. The station was

20 Finchley Road (Metropolitan Line) station c.1905, replaced 1913

reconstructed in 1934, when the old street building (31–33 High Holborn) was closed. This is still in existence and was formerly the entrance to a secret bunker.

The Central Line's **Holborn** platforms were opened on 25 September 1933 as the replacement for *British Museum*, providing an interchange with the Piccadilly line.

British Museum closed on the day the *Holborn* opened. During World War II the old station was used as an air raid shelter. The standard type of booking office building, on the north side of High Holborn, east of Bloomsbury Court, was pulled down in the late 1980s, but the white-tiled platforms may still be seen from the window of a passing train.

Tottenham Court Road. The original CLR street building lay outside Camden in Oxford Street, but the platforms lie partly in the borough. Since the 1920s the station has been entered by subways, most of whose entrances lie in the borough. Many of the wall surfaces are covered with mosaics designed by Eduardo Paolozzi.

Piccadilly Line

The next Tube to affect Camden was the Great Northern, Piccadilly and Brompton Railway, soon shortened to *Piccadilly*. This line opened on 15 December 1906, by which time all the Camden stations on the Piccadilly Line were open.

Stations

Holborn has an entrance set in a large office block which is contemporaneous with the railway. The station was extensively redecorated when it became an interchange with the Central Line in the 1930s.

Russell Square has the standard street building of Yerkes' Tube lines (Bakerloo, Piccadilly & Hampstead), designed by Leslie Green: ground and mezzanine floors with a flat roof, steel framed and clad in maroon (or 'liver-coloured') glazed blocks. The *art deco* lights and some of the tiling are not original. At platform level tiling in each station was arranged in coloured patterns unique to the station; Russell Square is a particularly good example, and still has the original direction signs incorporated in the tiling.

King's Cross was originally of the standard pattern for the line. The street building fronting Euston Road was removed around 1970 and the platform tiling also changed then.

Northern Line: City & South London

The Northern Line was created in the 1920s by the amalgamation of two separate railways: the City and South London (C&SLR) and the Hampstead Tube. The CSLR started life as a local line between the City of London and Stockwell. This was the first electric underground railway in the world when it opened in 1890. An extension to King's Cross and Euston via the Angel, Islington opened on 12 May 1907. A further extension connecting the C&SLR to the Hampstead Tube at Camden Town opened on 20 April 1924.

Stations

King's Cross. The C&SLR station was entered via a subway opening on the corner of Euston Road and Pancras Road. The station has been rebuilt both above and below ground. **Euston** had a surface building on the corner of Eversholt (formerly Seymour) Street and Doric Way (formerly Drummond Street) which was in use until 1914. Designed by Sidney Smith, this was faced in white and bore a passing resemblance to the famous Michelin building in Fulham. Only the ground floor was erected, although three more were planned. The building was pulled down in the 1930s. The original island platform was converted to an abnormally wide side-platform for southbound City branch trains when the Victoria Line was built.

Northern Line: Hampstead Tube

The other component of today's Northern Line was the Hampstead Tube. Opening on 22 June 1907, this was the last of the Edwardian Tubes, and the last entirely new line in Central London for 60 years. All the stations in Camden were available for use on the opening day. Along with the Hampstead Junction Railway and the North London, this line may be considered to be Camden's own.

Stations

Tottenham Court Road lies only partly in Camden. For the first year this station was known, rather more accurately than at present, as *Oxford Street*. A subsurface booking hall is approached by subways (there were never any surface buildings for the Hampstead Tube station here).

Goodge Street has the standard surface building (*cf. Russell Square*,

the major difference being the use of black letters on white to spell the station name on the cornice, a practice used throughout the Hampstead Tube). Known as *Tottenham Court Road* until 1908. **Warren Street**. The entrance is set into an early 1930s office block designed by Stanley Heaps. On the platform tiling the original name *Euston Road* (used for just under a year) may be glimpsed. **Euston**'s street building designed by Leslie Green, not used since 1914, can still be seen on the corner of Drummond and Melton Streets. **Mornington Crescent** remained for many years almost unchanged, was then closed for many years for refurbishment during the 1990s, and reopened much refreshed in 1999. **Camden Town**. The street building, of standard Green design, was partly destroyed by a bomb in 1940. A gap on the Chalk Farm Road side can still be seen. Since the advent of Camden Lock Market the station has become inadequate to local needs, and has frequently been closed or used for exit only at weekends.

Chalk Farm has an unnecessarily lengthy façade of standard type. **Belsize Park** is again of the standard design, which has survived intact since it opened [21, p 42]. **Hampstead** is the deepest on the Underground (192 feet). Recent refurbishment of the tiling has revealed the originally intended name, *Heath Street*, on some platform walls. **South Kentish Town** closed on 5 June 1924. The building is in use as a shop.

Kentish Town shares facilities with the adjacent Thameslink station.

Victoria Line

The section of the Victoria Line in Camden was opened from Highbury to Warren Street on 1 December 1968 and then from Warren Street to Victoria on 7 March the following year.

Stations

King's Cross St Pancras was worked into the existing station that served the Piccadilly and Northern Lines. **Warren Street.** The pictorial emblem on the platform tiling is a maze representing a warren, this being a rebus on the eponymous Anne Warren, wife of local landowner Charles Fitzroy (Lord Southampton). **Euston.** Cross-platform interchange is available with the City-bound Northern line trains. The platform tiling features the Euston Arch.

Jubilee Line

Before World War II the Metropolitan had a problem: between Finchley Road and Baker Street a bottleneck existed in the form of a two-track tunnel. Opening on 20 November 1939, a branch of the Bakerloo from Baker Street to Finchley Road took over Metropolitan local traffic as far as Stanmore, allowing the Metropolitan to run express services to more distant suburbs. The difficulty of the junction at Baker Street was solved by building a new line to Charing Cross, and transferring the Bakerloo's Stanmore branch to it. This was named in accord with the expected year of opening – 1977, Queen Elizabeth's Silver Jubilee – but it did not go into service until 1 May 1979.

Stations

Swiss Cottage still features the original décor of 1939 in the *art deco*

21 Belsize Park station, 1907, not long after opening but virtually the same today

pioneered by Charles Holden. Additional work was carried out in the 1960s.

Finchley Road and **West Hampstead** *see* Metropolitan Line stations, p 39.

Annotated bibliography for section 4

General: The literature on the Underground is immense. The general works quoted below are only those I found the most useful. Laurence Menear's book is an excellent survey of station architecture, although there are others of similar merit. The pamphlet by Pennick is a comprehensive account of the Tube shelters.

Subsurface lines: Jackson's book on the 'Met' is excellent but does not cover the post-1933 history of the line. The article "Railway connections at King's Cross" is a comprehensive account of the complex and fascinating history of the Metropolitan's links to other railways at King's Cross. An atmospheric account of work in the Midland Junction signal box in this area is in the May 1907 article.

Tube lines: The article "Recalling British Museum" in the London Railway Record *is an expanded version of the entry in J E Connor's book on closed Underground stations.*

Books
General
Derek A Bayliss, *The Post Office Railway* (Turntable publications, 1978)

Nigel Pennick, *Bunkers under London* (Valknut publications, 1988)

Laurence Menear, *London's Underground stations* (Midas books, 1993)

J E Connor, *London's disused Underground stations* (Connor & Butler, 2000)

Sub-surface lines (Circle & Metropolitan lines)
Alan A Jackson, *London's Metropolitan Railway* (David & Charles, 1986)

Tube lines (Central, Piccadilly, Northern, Victoria, Jubilee)
Mike Horne & Bob Bayman, *The first Tube* (Capital Transport, 1990)

M A C Horne, *The Victoria Line: a short history* (Douglas Rose, 1988)

M A C Horne, *The Jubilee Line* (Capital Transport, 2000)

Articles
Sub-surface lines
"Tunnel junctions" in *Railway Magazine*, May 1907

"Railway connections at King's Cross" in *Railway Magazine*, May and June 1962

Tube lines
"Recalling British Museum" in *London Railway Record*, Jan 1999

5 Locomotive depots & goods stations

The location of locomotive depots during the 19th century was influenced by two competing factors: they should be as near as possible to the point of use (e.g. termini), but the high price of land in the centre of the city obliged them to be some distance out.

Both the Midland and North Western companies located their original locomotive depots (Kentish Town and Camden) some way from the main London terminus (St Pancras and Euston), but these locations were at important junctions and also had major goods facilities nearby. King's Cross is somewhat exceptional in having its engine sheds almost adjacent to the passenger terminal.

Towards the latter part of the Victorian age the locomotive depots in Camden began to deal almost exclusively with passenger (especially express passenger) engines, and goods locomotives were housed elsewhere. Expansion in the, by now, built-up surroundings of the original sheds would clearly have been expensive. A similar process had been at work in relation to goods traffic, and the large marshalling yards needed to cope with the increased goods traffic had also had to be built outside the suburban area (Midland at Cricklewood, LNWR at Willesden and GNR at Hornsey). New sheds were therefore erected at these locations. These dealt mainly with goods engines, but local passenger locomotives tended to be housed there too.

Factors affecting the siting of goods depots were much the same as for locomotive facilities. Goods stations at Camden, King's Cross and St Pancras became collection and distribution centres, forwarding and receiving goods to and from the main shunting yards.

While they lasted, the goods depots and locomotive facilities provided a great deal of employment to the people of Camden, but in the middle of a densely populated area the smoke and dirt of the railways created an unattractive and unhealthy environment.

Camden

The area south of Chalk Farm Road was an important one for the London & Birmingham Railway. Initially it was to have been the London terminus of the railway, but an extension to the north side of Euston Square was soon authorised. The gradients on this extension were particularly steep since it was decided to go over the Regent's Canal and then to return to ground level at Euston. For almost the first seven years of the railway's life, therefore, passenger carriages were detached from their locomotives and then trundled down 'Camden Bank' to the station. Cables powered by stationary engines were used to haul carriages leaving Euston up the steeply graded Camden Bank. At the top, locomotives were attached for the run to the north. This spot was therefore the logical site for the locomotive depot, despite its high-class residential nature. The stationary engines were removed in 1844, but the basement of the engine house remains to this day. Cable haulage was really rather unnecessary even before 1844, indeed for the first three months after the line opened locomotive haulage was used as a 'temporary' emergency method since the stationary engines were not ready. The use of cable haulage may reflect uncertainty regarding the capability of steam locomotives rather than a weakness of the technology itself.

The original engine shed stood to the east of the main line, but did not last long because of the rapid increase in traffic. A magnificent new circular shed, designed by R B Dockray for goods engines, replaced it in 1847. After 1871 this shed was used as a warehouse. Since 1964 it has been used off and on as an arts centre, "The Round House", and there are current plans for a major refurbishment in a continuation of that role.

A shed for passenger engines, also dating from the late 1840s, stood to the west of the main line [22]. This was of conventional design and, with alterations, lasted almost until the depot's closure in the 1960s. After the opening of Willesden shed in 1873, Camden was used almost exclusively by the large express passenger locomotives, and was thus a Mecca for train buffs. Steam lasted until 1962, but the diesels did not stay long and the shed was closed completely on 3 January 1966. Today, carriage sidings occupy much of its site. An important relic of the locomotive depot is the former

22 Camden shed viewed from the south (c.1880)

enginemen's hostel of 1928, now used as flats, overlooking the line west of the Regent's Park Road bridge. These hostels were used as overnight accommodation for firemen and drivers and provided cooking and recreational facilities as well as beds.

The railway company's goods depot was also laid out here. The first construction that was brought into use around 1839, a series of embanked sidings in a very pretty pattern, lasted a very short time, as the North London was built through its site in the late 1840s. The main goods shed, overlooking the canal and abutting the main line, was built in 1864 and extended in the 1930s. A late addition of 1901–5 was the four-storeyed 'interchange warehouse' built over a dock of the Regent's Canal once picturesquely known as 'Dead Dog hole'. This building sheltered the transfer of goods from railway to barges transport and vice versa. The spirit merchants W & A Gilbey had extensive rail-served premises around the goods station. These included 'A' Shed (built c.1858) south of the canal and several warehouses, including

the former roundhouse mentioned above. Camden goods depot, like its passenger counterpart, was a hodgepodge of buildings of various ages and uses, but unlike at Euston there has been no grand rebuilding. The principal edifice was demolished and a supermarket was built on the site in the late 1990s. Most of Gilbey's accommodation met a similar fate, but other structures still stand, including the Interchange Building (now rather grand offices) and the stables with the associated horse hospital (1854–6, extended 1881), the latter currently in use as market premises (*Stables Market*).

Kentish Town

The land bordered by the Gospel Oak–Barking and Hampstead Junction lines, Highgate Road and Holmes Road saw extensive railway activity. South of the main line to St Pancras were numerous sidings, substantial goods and coal depots, and cattle pens for nearby Caledonian Market. A further large area was taken up by connecting lines to the Tottenham & Hampstead Junction. Outlying railway works in this area included an electricity

23 Highgate Road Enginemen's lodgings (1896), which served the Kentish Town sheds

generating station and an enginemen's lodging house [23], a grim edifice of 1896 to the east of Highgate Road (south of the railway, east of College Lane). The main facility in this locale, however, was the locomotive depot.

This was the Midland Railway's passenger engine depot and was opened along with the line in 1867–68. Like the LNWR's 'Camden' (Chalk Farm) depot, this was the company's only London depot before goods engines were relocated later in the 19th century (Cricklewood being the main Midland goods engine depot). Kentish Town was mostly used for express passenger locomotives but a number of tank engines, especially those fitted with condensing apparatus for local passenger trains travelling to Moorgate via the City Widened lines, were also based here. Originally, two sheds were provided. When the main line was widened in the 1890s one of these was demolished and in 1898 two new ones were erected. The remaining 1860s shed had a corner cut off to facilitate the passage of a new connecting line to the T&HJR. In 1939–40 modernisation resulted in new coal and ash plants. In the 1950s the sheds had to be re-roofed after bomb damage in World War II. With the dieselisation of the St

24 King's Cross goods: interior of shed as originally laid out in 1853

Pancras main line in the early 1960s the depot was rendered redundant, and it closed early the following year. Many of the buildings remain and are in non-railway use.

King's Cross

King's Cross is probably the best remaining example of a large Victorian goods station in England. The main remnant is the huge brick building known as 'the Granary' [24]. This dates from 1851 and was designed by Lewis Cubitt, the architect of the passenger and goods stations, the railway hotel and the original engine shed. The Granary has six floors and was originally devoted to the storage of goods – mainly, as the name would imply, of grain – but also had facilities for the transfer of goods to road transport and canal boats. Behind and to either side of the Granary are further 1850s buildings associated with trans-shipment facilities. The goods office is also of this date. Other goods structures still in situ include the 'Western Goods Shed' of 1897–99 and a pair of coal drops.

The main King's Cross locomotive depot, known as 'Top Shed' was to be found in this area, and was entirely surrounded by the goods department. The original engine shed of 1850 was an arc-shaped building, sometimes called 'the Crescent'. This was used for maintenance after 1862 when a conventional shed, subsequently known as the 'main line running shed' was built in front. A true 'roundhouse' was constructed to the north-east in 1859 for use by the Midland Railway (which ran trains into King's Cross until 1868). This was subsequently used for Great Northern suburban tank engines. Around 1900, goods engines were transferred to Hornsey, and King's Cross became the place to see big express passenger locomotives like the famous 'Flying Scotsman'. The depot was modernised in the early 1930s with new water-softening and coaling plants replacing the 'Midland Roundhouse', and in 1949 the 1860s shed was reconstructed after bomb damage. Main-line services were converted to diesel in the early 1960s, the new engines being housed in a new depot near Finsbury Park. The last steam engine was moved out in 1963 and the locomotive depot was closed and demolished. Although almost nothing remains of the shed itself many of the associated offices, such as the Locomotive Superintendent's House, still exist.

A secondary engine depot was located next to the passenger terminus. This was 'Bottom Shed', although for most of its life it had no undercover engine accommodation. From 1862 a shed was provided alongside the suburban station (see pp 15–16). This was demolished in 1893, but facilities for turning and fuelling engines continued to be provided in this area. After the expansion of the suburban station in 1924 a turntable and coaling stage were provided west of the main line, between the entrance to the Gas Works Tunnels and the station. This area was used for refuelling diesel engines from the early 1960s until 1980.

St Pancras

The Midland Railway goods facilities swallowed up huge tracts of land. As at King's Cross, these were mainly to the west of the main line, but here were divided between two sites: alongside the Regent's Canal by the North London line (referred to as 'Agar Town'); and near the passenger station ('Somers Town').

Agar Town goods depot opened on 2 January 1865 (built after more or less forced purchase of a small town built on land owned by the widow of William Agar and then completely demolished by the company). Until the main line was completed in 1868, access was via the North London or Great Northern Railway. The goods shed dated from that time, and from the late 1880s dealt mostly with incoming goods (i.e. arriving by rail from the north). Other facilities included a coal depot and, south of the canal, a Bass ale warehouse. The latter, called the Granary, was a huge building of roughly triangular plan, which became Woolworths' London depot in 1920.

During World War II the main goods shed was severely damaged by bombing; after being repaired, it continued in use until the 1960s. The area is now used as an industrial estate together with the Elm Village housing estate.

Somers Town goods yard was opened on 1 November 1887 but was not completed for another decade or

25 Somers Town goods station – exterior of milk and fish shed (1888)

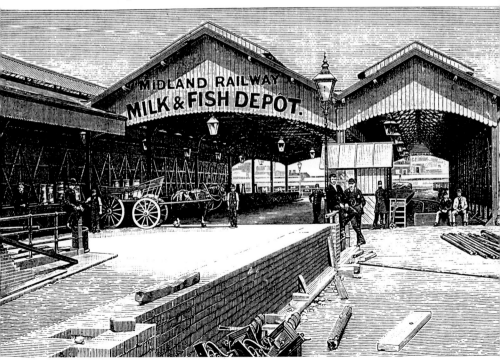

so. This was a huge complex on two levels bordered by Euston Road, Midland Road, Phoenix Street (now Brill Place) and Ossulston Street. It included within these bounds a coal depot, facilities for milk and fish distribution [25], a warehouse, a vegetable market (mostly handling potatoes and bananas), with appropriate offices for dealers and so on, as well as a general goods shed, which handled mostly outgoing traffic (i.e. from London). To the north was Purchese Street coal depot, in use from 1898 to 1968. Across the main road was a further coal depot known as 'Pancras Road'. Here was a coal drop – where coal was dropped, causing some breakage, from rail level into coal merchants' wagons below. The Pancras Road coal drop was rebuilt in the 1950s and is extant in almost complete form. Across the road is the brick façade of the Purchese Street depot.

On either side of former Cambridge Street in Agar Town were two further coal drops. That on the west was Midland's drop, and is now a refuse depot. On the eastern side were the rival GNR drops, which wagons approached from the east by way of a viaduct, then a bridge over the Regent's Canal. This has become Camley Street Natural Park, with few traces of railway interest surviving except for the ornate gates which were, laudably but confusingly, salvaged from the Midland Railway's Somers Town goods depot.

Somers Town depot was severely damaged by bombing in World War II, but remained in use until the late 1960s. The new British Library is now on the site. For the time being (early 2002), part of the neat multi-coloured brickwork of the perimeter walls remains to the north of the site.

Annotated bibliography for section 5

Camden: *The engine shed is described in the relevant section of vol.1 of Hawkins & Reeve's survey of LMS engine sheds (pp 82–88) and the hostel is featured in the well-illustrated article in the* Railway Magazine *of 1928. The* Illustrated London News *of 1847 features a superb engraving of the interior of the circular shed. Michael Robbins wrote a short biography of Dockray, the designer of this shed, for the* Camden History Review *of 1980. Its recent history as a cultural centre is outlined in Jinny Schiele's 1992 article for the same journal. Nothing of note seems previously to have been published specifically on Camden goods, although the 1864* Engineer *article is an excellent contemporary descriptive piece; however, a good account can be found in Jack Whitehead's book.*

Kentish Town: *The locomotive depot also appears in Hawkins & Reeve's series (vol.2, pp 118–124), this time in greater depth. The hostel was briefly featured in the* LMS Magazine *and in more detail in* The Engineer. *The GLIAS article on the Holmes Road coal depot is a description of structures then remaining on the site.*

King's Cross: *The goods station is particularly well covered.* Change at King's Cross *contains a brilliant archaeological survey of the King's Cross goods yard site on the eve of what appeared to be its final days,*

whilst the 1853 Illustrated London News *and the 1900* Railway Magazine *items are valuable contemporary descriptions of facilities at King's Cross. Townend's book covers the history of the shed in some detail; a briefer account is available in the book on GNR engine sheds.*
St Pancras: *The* British Railway Journal *article on St Pancras goods depots is excellent for its historical details, particularly in its depiction of the routine work of a large goods station in the pre-Grouping era, but does not cover more recent events in as much detail.* The Engineer *of 1888 features detailed plans and engravings of the Somers Town complex.*

Books
Camden
C Hawkins & G Reeve, *LMS engine sheds*, vol.1: *LNWR* (Wild Swan Publications, 1981)

Sarah Nelson, *History of the Camden goods yard* (unpublished thesis, 1986)

Jack Whitehead, *The growth of Camden Town* (pub: Jack Whitehead, 1999)

Kentish Town
C Hawkins & G Reeve, *LMS engine sheds*, vol.2: *Midland* (Wild Swan Publications, 1981)

King's Cross
R Griffiths & J Hooper, *GNR engine sheds*, vol.1: *Southern area* (Irwell Press, 1989)

M Hunter & R Thorne (eds), *Change at King's Cross* (Historical Publications, 1990)

P N Townend, *Top Shed* (Ian Allen, 1975)

Articles
Camden
"Great circular engine-house…" in *Illustrated London News*, 4 December 1847

"A railway goods station" in *The Engineer*, 7 October 1864

"Handling of traffic…Camden Yard" in *LMS Railway Magazine*, November 1928

"Enginemen's hostel at Chalk Farm, LMSR" in *Railway Magazine*, December 1928

"A Hampstead Victorian" in *Camden History Review* 8 (1980)

"The Round House, Chalk Farm" in *Camden History Review* 17 (1992)

Kentish Town
"The…Enginemen's Home…" in *The Engineer*, 16 April 1897

"Highgate Road enginemen's barracks" in *LMS Railway Magazine*, October 1924

"Midland Railway coal drops, Holmes Road…" in *Greater London Industrial Archaeology Society Newsletter*, August 1986

King's Cross
"The Great Northern Railway" (King's Cross) in *Illustrated London News*, 28 May 1853

"King's Cross goods station" in *Railway Magazine*, April 1900

St Pancras
"New St Pancras goods station" in *The Engineer*, 6 April 1888

"Goods traffic at St Pancras" in *British Railway Journal*, Spring 1993

Index

Passenger station names are *italicised*.
Boldface page numbers indicate main entries.
An asterisk* denotes inclusion of an illustration.

HJR = Hampstead Junction Railway;
Met = Metropolitan Railway.
For other abbreviations, see p 6.

54